MW00966725

MUSLIMS IN OUR COMMUNITY AND AROUND THE WORLD

A Supplementary Social Studies Unit for Grade Two

Written by Susan Douglass
Illustrated by Mahnaz Karimi

Goodwordkidz

Helping you build a family of faith

First published 1995 by
The International Institute of Islamic Thought (IIIT)
500 Grove St., 2nd Floor
Herndon, VA 20170-4735, USA
Tel: (1-703) 471 1133 / Fax: (1-703) 471 3922
E-mail: iiit@iiit.org / URL: http://www.iiit.org

First published by Goodword Books in 2003
Reprinted 2004
in arrangement with The International Institute of Islamic Thought
© The International Institute of Islamic Thought 1995

The Student Information/Text enclosed herein may be reproduced for
noncommercial educational purposes without obtaining prior written
permission from the copyright holder.

Goodword Books Pvt. Ltd.
1, Nizamuddin West Market
New Delhi 110 013
e-mail: info@goodwordbooks.com
Printed in India

www.goodwordbooks.com

Islamic School Book Project

IIIT is a cultural and intellectual foundation registered in the United States of America in 1981 with the objectives of providing a comprehensive Islamic outlook through elucidating the principle of Islam and relating them to relevant issues of contemporary thought; regaining the intellectual, cultural, and civilizational identity of the ummah through Islamization of the various disciplines of knowledge, to rectify the methodology of contemporary Islamic thought in order to enable it to resume its contribution to the progress of human civilization and give it meaning and direction in line with the values and objectives of Islam.

IIIT seeks to achieve its objectives by holding specialized academic seminars and conferences, supporting educational and cultural institutions and projects, supporting and guiding graduate and post-graduate studies.

The IIIT Islamic School Book Project supports the writing, publication, and distribution of books and other teaching material for schools as part of its effort to present the true picture of Islam in a factual objective way. These educational resources, developed under the general guidelines of the IIIT Islamization of Knowledge program, cover the following fields: Islamic Studies, Social Studies, Literature, Science and Mathematics. International collaboration and coordination with teachers, schools and organizations is assured through the International Forum for Education Resources for Islamic English-medium schools.

For more information contact:

The Director
IIIT Islamic School Book Project
International Institute of Islamic Thought (IIIT)
500 Grove St., 2nd Floor,
Herndon, VA 20170-4735, USA
Tel: (1-703) 471 1133 / Fax: (1-703) 471 3922
E-mail: iiit@iiit.org / URL: http://www.iiit.org

ABOUT THE AUTHOR

Susan Douglass is an American-born Muslim who accepted Islam in 1974. She received the Bachelor of Arts in History from the University of Rochester in 1972. She received the Master of Arts in Arab Studies from Georgetown University in 1992. She holds teaching certification in social studies from New York and Virginia.

She has taught in a variety of settings and subjects, beginning with volunteer work in Headstart in 1965. She taught and coordinated art classes in a summer youth program from 1970-79 in Rochester, NY. Since returning to the U.S. in 1984, from extended stays in Germany and Egypt, she resumed work in education. She has taught arts, crafts and story sessions in Muslim summer school programs for several years in Herndon, VA. As teacher and Head of the Social Studies Department at the Islamic Saudi Academy, Fairfax, VA, she taught both elementary and secondary social studies, built a supplementary resource library, and led in preparing a K-12 social studies curriculum utilizing both American and Arab resources for the Academy's accreditation. The current IIIT project was conceived and developed in the classroom. The author is involved in numerous other educational projects, including work as reviewer and consultant to major textbook publishers in the field of social studies. She has reviewed and offered revisions to the California History/Social Science Framework (1994) and the National History Standards Project (1994), in addition to various projects for the Council on Islamic Education in Fountain Valley, CA, including a book, *Strategies and Structures for Presenting World History, with Islam and Muslim History as a Case Study* (Council on Islamic Education, 1994.)

ADVISORY PANEL MEMBERS

Rahima Abdullah
Elementary Coordinator
Islamic Saudi Academy, Alexandria, VA

Dr. Kadija A. Ali
Educational Projects Coordinator
International Institute of Islamic Thought, Herndon, VA

Jinan N. Alkhateeb
Social Studies Teacher
Islamic Saudi Academy, Alexandria, VA

Mrs. Hamida Amanat
Director of Education
American Islamic Academy
Curriculum Consultant
Al-Ghazaly School, Pine brook, NJ

Shaker El Sayed
Coordinator
Islamic Teaching Center, Islamic Schools Department
Islamic Society of North America, Plainfield, IN

Dr. Tasneema Ghazi
IQRA International Educational Foundation, Chicago, IL

Dr. Zakiyyah Muhammad
Universal Institute of Islamic Education, Sacramento, CA

4

Many people's efforts have contributed to producing this series of supplementary units for Social Studies. First, I am grateful to the International Institute of Islamic Thought (IIIT) for placing their confidence in me to undertake a project of this size and for providing all the financial and logistical resources needed for its completion. I would like to thank Dr. Mahmud Rashdan, under whose guidance this project began in 1988. His wisdom helped to set it on a solid foundation. Without constant support and encouragement by Dr. Omar Kasule, project director 1991-present, and Dr. Khadija Ali Sharief, project coordinator (1993-present), this unit would never have met the light of day.

The project has been much enhanced by the members of the Advisory Panel. In addition to offering guidance on the project as a whole, they have spent time and detailed effort on each individual manuscript. These brothers and sisters are all active education professionals with a broad range of experience and a long list of accomplishments.

May Allah reward my family and grant them patience for sacrificing some degree of comfort so that I, as wife and mother, might realize this goal. I owe special thanks to my husband, Usama Amer, for his constant help with the computer, with Arabic sources and many other matters of consultation. With regard to the research, writing and editing process, I thank the children who contributed their ideas to the manuscript. Many members of the Muslim commmunity in the United States also donated their time, allowing me to visit their workplaces to discuss their jobs and take photographs. Several Muslim organizations, such as the Islamic Society of North America and the Islamic Center in Washington, D.C. and several Muslim schools have also contributed photographs. Gratitude is extended to Rabiah Abdullah, whose keen mind and sharp pencil have shaped and pruned text for the whole project as well as lending her encouragement since its inception. The illustrator, Mahnaz Karimi, worked skillfully and independently from halfway across the U.S. under pressure of the deadline. Finally, thanks to the many people of Kendall-Hunt Publishing Co. who graciously met my many requests and turned tentative, complex and unfamiliar material into a finished product.

May Allah reward the efforts of sincere workers and of the teachers and students for whom this unit was written.

Susan Douglass
Falls Church, Virginia
December 1994

Part I

Introduction for the Teacher

Part II

Part III

Part IV

Student Activities

Part I:

Introduction for the Teacher

INTRODUCTION

This unit is the third in a series of units for use in Muslim school Social Studies programs. The underlying assumption is that many or most such schools will use mainstream curriculula as a starting point. While it is certainly desirable and necessary to produce a complete Islamic Social Studies curriculum, it is a task which is best taken on step-by-step. In the meantime, it seems most productive to design supplements which are integrated into topics typically studied at a given grade level, while introducing content vital to the development of Muslim identity, values and world view. At the same time, it is hoped that the issues covered in these units are of such importance that they might in turn become integrated into a complete Islamic curriculum.

An important requirement in the design of this supplementary series is that each unit features skills and concepts typical for the scope and sequence of the social studies curriculum in its grade level. In this way, the teacher can introduce information about the Islamic heritage using material that is well integrated into the existing social studies program. This feature of the design also makes it possible to substitute this material for unsatisfactory or unnecessary material from standard textbooks, thus avoiding overburdening the students.

PURPOSE

The purpose of the unit is to cultivate an understanding that Muslims everywhere practice Islam in similar ways, and that they need communities to help them follow Islam. Beginning with a description of a Muslim home, the unit is developed beyond the home to the activities carried on by Muslim individuals outside the home, including service to the larger community and participation in the Muslim community through the masjid. Muslim countries and transplanted or indigenous Muslim communities in non-Muslim countries are described, and the links which unite them are explored on the levels of religious duty, customs and co-operation. A brief introduction to the geography of Muslim countries is given.

Corollary to an understanding that Muslims need communities is the concept that Muslims bear the responsibility to develop their community. The lessons show how Muslims work together to make sure that it provides those services which are a part of compliance with Islamic law (Shari'ah). Finally, the lessons in this unit are intended to foster a sense of identity for children living in non-Muslim communities. It is intended to show that the "differentness" of the Muslim from his surroundings goes beyond custom and taste. The central fact of the Muslim community's identity is its adherence to Islam.

"Muslims in Our Community and Around the World," is intended as a supplement to the typical second grade curriculum study of communities.

CHAPTER 1 — MUSLIMS IN OUR COMMUNITY

- Section 1 describes a Muslim home and the normal activities therein.
- Section 2 describes what family members do outside the home to maintain it and to serve the community in an Islamic manner. It also describes some Muslim businesses which provide needed services and products.
- Section 3 discusses attendance at the masjid and the activities that take place there.
- Section 4 describes how people in the community help each other to follow Islam. It tells how the community works together to meet its needs, and how it obtains resources for service projects.
- Section 5 describes the family's preparation for a trip to the home country of the parents to visit their relatives, and how other Muslim families plan the same kind of journey.

CHAPTER 2 — MUSLIMS AROUND THE WORLD

- Section 6 provides introductory information about the geographic features of Muslim communities.
- Section 7 discusses some types of Muslim communities, from urban to rural.
- Section 8 defines and describes Muslim countries.
- Section 9 talks about other countries where Muslims live, tells how they are different from Muslim countries, and why Muslims live there, as well as discussing Muslims who are native to non-Muslim countries.

Each lesson is accompanied by supplementary activities. The complete unit is designed for 10-12 class periods. Conceptual reinforcement, as well as practice with maps and diagrams are included. Several activities integrate language arts and fine arts. Two field trips, a project and a suggested class visitor offer enrichment.

CHAPTER 1: MUSLIMS IN OUR COMMUNITY

SECTION 1: A Muslim Family at Home
The student will
- list some daily duties of Muslims
- list other things Muslims do to please Allah (SWT) at home
- define *halal* food
- describe how Muslims should receive guests
- define and give examples of custom(s)

SECTION 2: Following Islam Outside the Home
The student will
- describe how Muslims should behave in public
- tell where Muslims can buy *halal* foods
- list some services based on custom and preference
- list some jobs which help in the community
- tell how Muslims share their products and services with others
- define business as a seller of services or products

SECTION 3: In the Masjid
The student will
- tell who goes to a masjid
- define Islamic law
- tell why Muslims follow Islamic laws
- list some activities that take place in the masjid
- list some Islamic occasions for celebration

SECTION 4: Helping in the Community
The student will
- define community as people living and working together
- describe the Muslim community's goals and needs
- list ways the community works together to meet its needs
- tell how Muslim communities find resources to meet needs
- explain how resources are used for projects and charity

SECTION 5: Trip to a Muslim Country
The student will
- define relative
- list some of his/her relatives by name and title
- tell where his/her relatives live

CHAPTER 2: MUSLIMS AROUND THE WORLD

SECTION 6: Where Muslims Live
The student will
- describe places where Muslims live
- explain that Muslim communities exist in various places

SECTION 7: Muslim Communities
The student will
- describe Muslim cities
- describe activities in a Muslim village
- compare use of animals and machines for farming
- explain why nomads move with their herds

SECTION 8: Muslim Countries
The student will
- use a map to identify Muslim countries
- define Muslim country
- list everyday things they would see in any Muslim country

SECTION 9: Living in Other Countries
The student will
- tell why and which Muslims live in non-Muslim countries
- list some activities of Muslims in those countries
- compare Muslim countries with non-Muslim countries
- list some customs from the country in which they live

Part II:

Student Text

MUSLIMS
IN OUR COMMUNITY
AND AROUND THE WORLD

Written by Susan Douglass
Illustrated by Mahnaz Karmi

وَٱعْتَصِمُوا بِحَبْلِ ٱللَّهِ جَمِيعًا وَلَا تَفَرَّقُوا

And hold fast,
All of you together,
To the rope of Allah,
And do not separate. (Qur'an 3:103)

CHAPTER 1:

Muslims in our Community

A Muslim Family at Home

This is a Muslim family. Here is father Abdullah. Here is mother Karima. The children's names are Muhammad, Amina and Maryam. They live and work together in this house. They help each other. They like to please Allah (SWT).

They pray five times each day. When everyone is at home, Abdullah says **adhan**. The family prays together. When father is not home, Karima prays with the children. Sometimes Muhammad leads prayer for his sisters.

The family learns together. They read Qur'an and Hadith. They read books together. They talk about the stories and books they read.

Each member of the family has jobs. They keep themselves and their house clean and beautiful. They help each other with this work.

Muslim families eat **halal** food. **Halal** means Allah (SWT) allows us to eat it. Muslims are not allowed to eat pork. Amina and Muhammad help prepare chicken.

Today an American Muslim family visits their home. The father Ishaq is a policeman. His wife Khadijah is a teacher. They have two children, Layla and Hassan.

Muslim families make their guests feel comfortable. They share food and drink with their guests. The children share toys with their visitors. Muhammad helps Father serve coffee in tiny cups. That is a **custom** in Abdullah's home country.

Section 1 Questions:

1. Name some things a Muslim family does to please Allah (SWT).
2. How often do Muslims pray? Do they pray together?
3. How do children help at home?

Following Islam Away From Home

The family members are busy away from home. Muhammad and Amina work hard in school. Karima is a physician. Abdullah owns a factory where books are made. They work to please Allah (SWT).

When they go outside, members of the family behave as Muslims. They don't argue or talk loudly. Abdullah and Karima drive the car very carefully. The children never litter the streets. They are always polite.

Today the family goes shopping. They stop at a **halal** butcher shop. Muslim butchers sell **halal** meat. They do not sell **pork**. Karima asks the butcher to cut the meat. He sells other things that Muslim families enjoy. The spices smell very nice! Maryam asks Mother to buy some incense. Burning incense is a **custom** in many Muslim homes. Amina buys a coloring book with Arabic letters. Abdullah buys Karima a pretty scarf.

Next door is a restaurant. The owner is Muslim. Muslim families go there to enjoy the delicious food. Many other American families like the restaurant, too.

The store and the restaurant buy bread from a bakery. Muslim bakers make flat bread in a factory. Muslim families like to eat this bread. So do other Americans. It is sold in the supermarket.

The family stops by Abdullah's office. The children like the noise of the big printing machines. Workers use computers and machines to print Arabic and English. They make books, magazines and newspapers. Printing helps people learn about Islam. It helps people learn about each other.

Nearby is the clinic where Karima works. She helps sick children get well. She helps them stay healthy.

Many Muslim workers and **businesses** help families. **Businesses** serve people. **Businesses** sell products, or things, to people. Can you name some businesses that help Muslims and others?

Section 2 Questions:

1. What do family members do outside their home?
2. How should Muslims behave outside their home?
3. Name some special foods your family enjoys.
4. Think of some jobs that help people.

In the Masjid

The family visits the **masjid** often. The **masjid** is a place where many Muslims pray. They enjoy meeting other Muslims. They help each other to please Allah (SWT).

They help each other follow **Islamic laws**. Islamic laws tell what Allah (SWT) wants Muslims to do. Muslims learn about Islamic laws from Qur'an and Hadith.

On Fridays, Muslim men must meet there for Juma'a prayer. Women and children pray Juma'a, too.

Families go to the **masjid** to learn and to teach others. Muslims teach their children to read the Qur'an. Adults also practice reading Qur'an together. They read other books and talk about important things at the masjid.

Muslims **celebrate** at the **masjid** with other families. They celebrate the two Islamic festivals, *'Id al-Fitr* and *'Id al-Adha*. Muslim families also celebrate weddings there. This family celebrates the birth of a new baby.

Muslims also tell visitors about Islam. They invite people to Islam.

Section 3 Questions:

1. Who goes to the **masjid**?
2. How do Muslims know about Islamic laws?
3. Name three activities in a **masjid**.
4. When do Muslim families celebrate together?

Helping to Build the Community

Wherever they live, Muslims help each other. They work together to please Allah (SWT). People and families working and living together are called **communities**. The community helps its members to be good Muslims.

The people in the community meet. They talk about the work they will do together. They meet to talk about the community's needs. Karima says they need a new school. Others want businesses and offices that help Muslim families. Muslim writers want to print books. The community helps to start the work.

The community decides to build an Islamic Center. Members of the community help to raise money. Some families cook food to sell to visitors. Some members make things to sell. Others spend time and money to help with the project.

The Muslim community also spends money to help needy people. Allah (SWT) told Muslims to do that. Some money helps needy people in the community. Money is sent to needy people in other countries, too.

Section 4 Questions:

1. What does a Muslim community need?
2. How does the community plan for its needs?
3. How is money used by the Muslim community?
4. What can you do to help your community serve Allah (SWT)?

Trip to a Muslim Country

The family decides to go on a trip. They will visit **relatives** in Abdullah's home country. The children's grandparents, aunts, uncles and cousins live in another country. The family will travel by airplane. Abdullah buys the tickets at a travel agency. When the big day comes, the family goes to the airport.

At the airport, they meet other Muslim families. They want to visit **relatives**. They will travel to many different places.

Section 5 Questions:

1. Name some of your relatives. Tell how each is related to you.
2. Where do your relatives live?

CHAPTER 2:
Muslims Around the World

Where Muslims Live

Muslims live in many different places. Many Muslims live where the weather is hot and dry. Some live near rivers or oceans. They live on cool mountains. They live on warm islands. There are Muslim communities in almost every kind of climate.

Section 6 Questions:

1. What is the climate like where you live?
2. Tell about the weather in one of the pictures.

Muslim Communities

Some Muslims live in large cities. Their homes and offices are in tall buildings. They work at many different jobs.

Some Muslims live in small communities called **villages**. Farmers in the village grow food and other crops. Others raise animals to sell. Animals also help with farm work. Many farmers use large machines.

In dry countries, some Muslims move their homes from place to place. They lead their animals to find grass and water. Animals and machines bring water to the dry land.

Section 7 Questions:

1. Name some jobs in a city.
2. How are animals used by the farmers?
3. Why do farmers use machines?

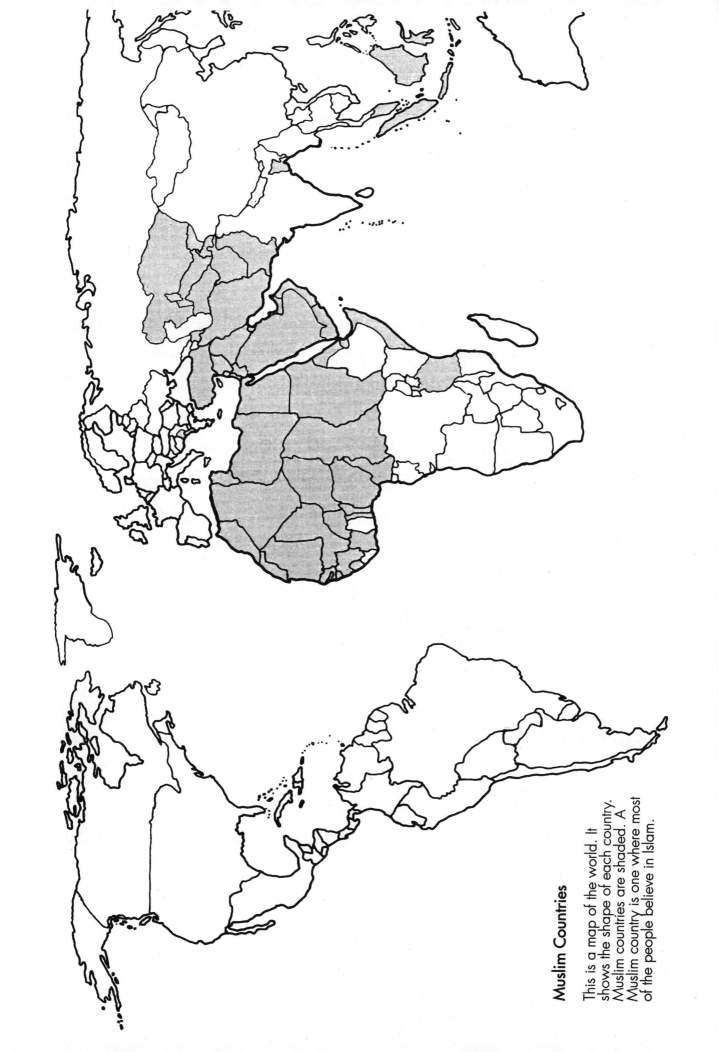

Muslim Countries

This is a map of the world. It shows the shape of each country. Muslim countries are shaded. A Muslim country is one where most of the people believe in Islam.

Muslim Countries

This is a map of the world. It shows the shape of each country. Muslim countries are shaded. A Muslim country is one where most of the people believe in Islam.

Islam is very important in the Muslim countries. Each community has many **masajid**. You can hear **adhan** five times each day in villages and cities. Children learn to read the Qur'an in school. You can see shows about Islam on television.

Many Muslims speak Arabic every day. Others speak different languages. All Muslims say their prayers in Arabic.

Section 8 Questions:

1. How many Muslim countries are shown on the map?
2. How could you travel to a Muslim country from your home?
3. Name some things you would see in a Muslim country.

Living in Other Countries

Muslims also live outside Muslim countries. Muslims travel to these countries for many reasons. They work at many jobs. They study in large schools called **universities**. Some Muslims teach in universities.

Many Muslims are also born in countries where most people are not Muslims. Some of the people become Muslims after learning about Islam.

Most people in those countries are not Muslim. They do not follow Islam. They follow different beliefs. They have different customs. They have different laws and governments.

Muslims follow Islam wherever they live. Muslims live all over the world.

Section 9 Questions:

1. Do you live in a Muslim country?
2. Are your parents from a Muslim country?
3. Why do Muslims travel to other countries?
4. How are Muslim countries different from other countries?

halal = things which are allowed by Allah (SWT)

pork = meat from the pig

business = place where people work to earn money. Businesses do work for people and sell products.

masjid = a building where Muslims pray

celebrate = to have a holiday or festival

restaurant = a business that cooks food for people

community = people and families living and working together

Islamic laws = what Allah (SWT) wants Muslims to do. We learn about Islamic laws from the Qur'an and Prophet Muhammad's ﷺ life.

relatives = members of your big family

Muslim country = a country where most people believe in Islam

village = a farming community

custom = something people like to do, a habit

Part III:

Teaching Suggestions & Supplementary Activities

The student text is illustrated with black-line coloring book pages. Each reproducible coloring page is designed to accompany a section of the text. Students are encouraged to study the scenes as they color; the class may also discuss the features of each scene. Some scenes will also be useful in answering the comprehension questions at the end of each section. In addition, a set of classroom posters is an integral part of the unit. Activities for each poster are described in the following teaching suggestions. A classroom set of laminated maps showing the Muslim countries may be ordered to accompany Poster #4.

CHAPTER 1: MUSLIMS IN OUR COMMUNITY

SECTION 1: A Muslim Family at Home

NOTE: One of the major themes of this unit is "doing things to please Allah (SWT)." Theme will be followed from the individual to the family level to the community level, and may be abstracted to the level of the nation by the teacher.

Pre-reading: Ask the class what they would expect to find in a Muslim home. What would the family members be doing?

Comprehension: In Section 1, discussion centers around what the members of the family do to please Allah (SWT), i.e., to follow Islam at home. The concepts of duties, customs and traditions are defined by example and contrasted with one another. In this connection, the word halal receives some attention in terms of family dietary choices. In the next section, more detailed attention will be given to the concept.

Putting concepts to work: List all of the things mentioned in the story which relate to following Islam. Expand the list by eliciting the students' own experiences at home. Concentrate in particular on the duties of each family member toward one another and toward Allah (SWT).

Defining new concepts: Draw the students' attention to the custom of coffee-drinking. Mention other customs common in Muslim homes, as well as some customs in American or other societies which the children have noticed. Holiday magazine pictures might help to illustrate these ideas, as well as picture books showing various traditional cultures such as Native-Americans, Africans, Asian peoples, etc.

NOTE: Another important objective of the unit is to draw a clear distinction in the children's mind between Islamic laws (or doing things which Allah (SWT) has ordered and avoiding those forbidden), which are related to pleasing Allah (SWT), and customs (things done because of preference, habit and tradition, which are religiously neutral).

SECTION 2: Following Islam Outside the Home

Pre-reading/Comprehension: Ask why each member of the family goes outside the home. What activities do they do? Which of these activities are important for the family? (working to earn money, going to school to learn, buying what the family needs) Which activities serve people outside the family? (working in jobs that help others) How do these activities serve Allah (SWT)?

Values Activity: Islamic manners are outlined very briefly here; expand the catalogue of excellent Muslim behavior in public by making a poster of these and further characteristics, using words and pictures.

Field Trip: Visit a halal butcher or grocery store in your area. Have the owner or manager talk to the class about how and where he gets the meat, and how it is different from the way a supermarket gets its supply. Have him also discuss the origin of groceries and other products which he sells. Have him tell about the people who come to buy from his store. Draw up a list of questions for the class to ask. As a follow-up activity, the children might illustrate a "Story of Our Halal Food" diagram or book.

Games and Fun: Share samples of special dishes or dessert treats enjoyed by Muslims of different lands. Have the children decorate labels for the country where it is enjoyed. This activity might be expanded to include traditional craft artifacts brought from home.

Putting Concepts to Work: Extend the above activity to further develop the concept of custom from Section 2. Build upon the purchase of a scarf mentioned in the story by discussing styles of dress among Muslims. If samples of Muslim dress can be collected from parents, display them on life-size cardboard paper dolls decorated by the class. Alternatively, make paper dolls to dress with paper replicas of Indo-Pakistani, Arab, Turkish, Malay, and various styles of African Muslim dress. Both traditional and modern dress could be represented. This provides an opportunity to illustrate the difference between Islamic law and custom. Explain very simply, for example, that Muslim women are required to cover their bodies and heads in a certain way. But the style and color of their dress is a custom, habit and preference which varies widely.

Map Activities: Draw a simple map of a Muslim community, using a legend to show where the masjid, the halal meat store, the school, etc. are located. Let the children invent symbols for the legend. The map might be mural size or individual work. A very energetic class might undertake a more sophisticated project to find out how many halal meat stores serve their community or metro area; how many masajid, how many Islamic schools of all kinds, and what other Islamic organizations are found there. These might be located on a street or road map keyed with colored flags or push pins. Local Muslim business directories or phone books might be available to help. This activity, since it will take a considerable amount of time, might be sustained throughout study of Chapter 1. See the variation and expansion mentioned as a map activity to accompany Section 7.

Putting Economic Concepts to Work: Develop a definition of business, using its root, "busy," to express work and activity. As the text paragraph explains, the object of businesses is to earn money for the workers by selling something, and to provide something needed or wanted by people who buy. Using examples from the story, ask the students what each business described is selling. (bread, meat, books, food, and in the case of the clinic, health care) Make a list of these things on the board, then add examples from other businesses, perhaps using the children's parents' professions as examples. Then try to categorize the things sold into goods and services. An interesting method is to ask which things could be put in a shopping bag, and which could not.

SECTION 3: In the Masjid

Crossover to Islamic studies: Make a list of Do's and Don'ts for behavior in the masjid. Discuss other aspects of etiquette in the masjid, such as saying a two-rakat prayer upon entry, etc.

Putting concepts to work: Discuss the origin of Islamic laws. (derived from Qur'an and Sunnah by the work of Muslim scholars over many years) Why do Muslims follow these laws? How are these laws different from other laws and rules? Build here on concepts presented in the regular textbook, for which this unit is a supplement. A very ambitious class might embark upon discussion of the kinds of laws people can decide upon by vote or concensus, and the kind which Allah (SWT) requires Muslims to follow.

Field Trip: Visit an Islamic Center, masjid or other Muslim institution in your community. Make an appointment for someone at the center to give the class a tour and answer questions which the class has formulated in discussion and written down. As a pre-activity, use Poster #1 to discuss what an Islamic center is. After the visit, have the children make a mural to illustrate activities in the center they visited. How is an Islamic Center different from, and the same as, a masjid?

Language Skills: Have the students write about their own visits to the masjid or Islamic Center. Do they go often? What does it look like? In what activities do they participate? What do they like most about visiting the masjid? Another writing topic, especially just after an 'Id celebration, would involve writing about how the child's family celebrates, including clothing, food and activities.

SECTION 4: Helping to Build the Community

Putting Concepts to Work: Expand upon the theme of "pleasing Allah (SWT)" by discussing the links between families and their members following Islam, and many families, or a community cooperating to make it easier to follow Islam, or to do things that one person or one family cannot do (like building a school or a masjid, or making books). The concept to be developed here by the teacher is that Allah (SWT) ordered Muslims to do certain things alone, but He also ordered Muslims to work together to form communities in order to complete their obedience to Him. Explain how Prophet Muhammad (SAAS) gave the Muslims an example of how to do that, because he was the leader of a large community.

Games and Fun: Charades — Have the children act out different services Muslims provide and need in their communities. They may play as teams or individuals.

Poster #2 Activity: Use the pattern provided in these notes to make a cardboard dial for the center of Poster #2. Attach at star with a paper fastener. Using the dial to cover each section, play a game to see who knows how each occupation on the chart helps Muslims to please Allah (SWT) and carry out Islamic laws.

Map Activity: Make or acquire an enlarged and simplified map of your city or community. Use different colored flags to locate masajid, Islamic schools, stores, and other important resources in your community. If they are clustered in certain areas, try to identify reasons. If scattered, what does that say about how large the community is in your area? Encourage the children to try out different ideas.

Values and Economic Concepts At Work: Discuss the statement in the text, "Others spend time and money to help with the project." The important concept here is the idea that some people offer money as a gift for a project, while others may offer their skills to work in any way that is needed. Explain that both are important resources for any community. That way, everyone can help somehow.

Finally, the sophisticated but basic economic concept of opportunity cost can be introduced by discussing what it means to give from your time, in other words, to spend time away from your family and regular job to help the community, or give up something we want in order to give money to others. These might mean giving up some free time and extra money, like not taking a vacation or going to the movies. It pleases Allah (SWT) when we give up some nice things for ourselves to help build the community. The word sacrifice might be reviewed in this connection if it is familiar to the students.

Putting concepts to work: Name some ways a community might raise money for projects. Have the students think about what kinds of people are needy. (Those with no money, the sick, old people, people suffering from war, those with not enough to eat, places where the weather makes life hard.)

Charity Project: Have the class make a project to collect money or things, or perform a service for some needy people. They may donate toys, collect cans or sell cookies at the masjid. They may volunteer a service to some group or individual in need. The children might benefit from involvement in the selection of a needy Muslim group or other charity (homeless, orphanage, etc.). Other suggestions include making story tapes for the blind, drawing pictures for sick or other unfortunate children. They may collect money to purchase a book for another Muslim school. The class could make a cassette or video tape and/or cards to go along with their gift, service or donation.

Language and Concept Skills Activity: (Linking Muslim Communities) Arrange to write letters to the 2nd grade class in another Muslim school in the U.S. If possible, include photos or illustrations of Muslim activities, centers and services in your community. Ask what is found in their community, and request similar letters and pictures. Other activites could follow from this interesting exchange project.

SECTION 5: Trip to a Muslim Country

Games and Fun: Increase awareness of relatives by reading the book Hooray for Me (Remy Charlip and Lilian Moore, Parents' Magazine Press, 1975), explaining how each of us carries many titles (son, cousin, brother, nephew) as a family member. As a follow-up, have each student work with parents at home to make a family tree of photographs of some relatives. The parents may just label the photos (father, mother, sister, cousin, etc.) and students may match them to similar labels on the tree in Worksheet #3, or parents may be encouraged to work with the child on a longer-term project to arrange them more formally on a poster or large paper.

Life Experience: Bring examples of an airline ticket to the classroom and discuss the preparations needed for a long trip like the one the story family is making. Discuss the cost for each family member, the way reservations are made, and even seats assigned and Muslim meals ordered by computer. Discuss what preparations the family makes at home (someone to watch the house, care for pets and plants, etc.) and for the people they will visit (buying presents, collecting photos, etc.).

CHAPTER 2: MUSLIMS AROUND THE WORLD

SECTION 6: Where Muslims Live

Putting concepts to work: Name some resources shown in the pictures. Tell how they are the same and different from those in other pictures. (See also Poster #3.)

Geography Skills: Ask the students to describe the weather in the pictures on Poster #3, and see what clues each picture gives about the kind of land and climate in those places.

SECTION 7: Muslim Communities

Compare and Contrast: Classify the pictures on Poster #3 and the coloring book illustrations as to which are more like "cities" or "villages." Ask why the students chose their answer, or what is the evidence for their conclusion.

Putting concepts to work: Name some ways these people use animals as a resource. Discuss how the living animal can help (raising water, transportation, milk), and how its meat, wool and leather can be used.

Geography skills: An enrichment activity related to this section involves the resources found in these countries and sold at home and in other countries. The teacher might discuss the agricultural products mentioned in the text, and build on that to discuss products taken from the ground, like metals, oil and gas, etc., as an introduction.

SECTION 8: Muslim Countries

Map Activity: Using a wall map and the coloring page for this section, help the children locate Muslim countries. Find out from which countries the children's parents or grandparents came. For practice in using directions, find out which direction (N,S,E,W) these countries lie relative to the class, and what transportation might be used to get to each.

Map Activity / Poster #3 Activity: Using a classroom globe or wall map, find the names of the countries shown in poster illustrations. Have a student point out and follow the line from each illustration. With the teacher's help, the other students can try to match the shape of the country and its location with the wall map. Discuss the climate or geographic features, and kind of community shown in each picture.

Geography Skills: Show the students a map or globe of Muslim countries, preferably from a laminated map set. Assign small groups of students a specific country in which they will count the dots which represent cities. If the map has smaller and larger dots, have them count the largest ones. Let the groups record the results of their search and present them to the class. The teacher can tally the results for each country on the board, then discuss which Muslim countries have many cities. A further expansion would involve guessing why some countries have more cities, and where many cities are found (on rivers, near oceans, etc.), or where few are found (near mountains and deserts).

SECTION 9: Living in Other Countries

Putting concepts to work: Further explore the concept of custom. Ask the children about special foods their family likes to eat, or certain kinds of clothes they wear. How are these things different from food and clothes of other Americans? Have the class list some American food and other customs (holidays, dress, etc.). Explore with the class why people might like certain things. How are customs different from laws? How are some customs of Muslims different from American customs? How are they the same?

Putting concepts to work: Make a chart with two columns, "Same" and "Different," comparing Muslim countries with other countries.

Class Visitor: Invite a parent or other individual who left the country where he was born to come to the U.S. Have him show pictures of his family members, his house, his village or city in the home country. He might explain for what purpose he came, describe his journey, and describe his feelings for his home. He might then tell the children how he found new Muslim friends and how the Muslim community helped him to settle in his new home.

> **Follow-up:**
> a. Later, the class could share similar anecdotes and photos from the students' own families.
> b. Each child might write and illustrate a story telling about his own parents' journey or other experience finding Muslim friends in the community.

REVIEW: Language and Concept Skills Activity: Sentence Chop-Ups — The sentences on Worksheet # 1 express key concepts in the text. Transfer them to overhead projector film or to the blackboard. Make an additional copy of the worksheet. Prepare as many envelopes as sentences, cutting up each sentence into separate words and placing the pieces in an envelope. After reading and discussing each sentence with the class, divide the class into groups, one per envelope. The group leader passes one or more words to each member of his group, and they figure out how to put the sentence back together. (After the teacher checks the answer,) the group glues its sentence on paper.

Part IV:

Student Activities

Section 1:

1. Name three things a Muslim family does to please Allah (SWT).
2. How often do the family members pray? Do they pray together?
3. How do children help at home?

KEY:

1. They pray, read Qur'an, eat halal food, keep their house clean and share with guests.
2. They pray five times. They usually pray together.
3. They help with cleaning and preparing food, and the older ones lead the prayer for younger children.

Section 2:

1. What do the family members do outside their home?
2. Name some special foods your family enjoys.
3. Who likes to buy special products from Muslims?
4. Make a list of five jobs or businesses that help people.

KEY:

1. They go to school and work and go shopping.
2. Answers vary.
3. Muslim families and American families buy these products.
4. Doctors, teachers, food stores, printing factories, restaurants, etc.

Section 3:

1. Who goes to the masjid?
2. Name three activities that take place in a masjid.
3. When do Muslim families celebrate together?

KEY:

1. Adults and children as well as visitors go.
2. Juma' prayer, learning to read Qur'an, learning and teaching about Islam,

celebrations.

3. They celebrate two Islamic holidays, weddings, and when a baby is born

Section 4:

1. How does the community plan for its needs?
2. Name three services which Muslim communities need.
3. How do Muslim communities use money to serve Allah (SWT)?

KEY:

1. People have meetings to talk and make plans.
2. They need places to pray, schools, food stores, clothes, doctors, etc.
3. Communities use money for projects they need, and they give money to needy people.

Section 5:

1. Name some of your relatives. Tell how each is related to you.
2. Where do your relatives live?

KEY:

1. Answers vary.
2. Answers vary.

Section 6:

1. What is the climate like where you live?
2. Tell about the weather in one of the pictures.

KEY:

1. Answers vary.
2. Answers vary, but should include information about hot and cold, wet and dry.

Section 7:

1. Name some jobs in a Muslim city.
2. How are animals used by the farmers?
3. Why do the farmers also use machines?

KEY:

1. Office worker, transportation worker, doctor, teacher, producer in a factory, policeman, fireman, etc.
2. They are used to do work and to sell for meat, milk and leather.
3. Machines do the work faster than people or animals.

Section 8:

1. How many Muslim countries are shown on the map?
2. How could you travel to a Muslim country from your home?
3. Name three things you would see in a Muslim country.

KEY:

1. See map, p.36.
2. You could travel by boat or airplane.
3. Masajid, Arabic signs, Muslim dress, people praying together.

Section 9:

1. How are Muslim countries different from other countries?
2. Why do Muslims travel to other countries?
3. Do some Muslims live outside Muslim countries?

KEY:

1. Most people in other countries don't believe in Islam. The people have different customs.
2. They travel to work, to study and to teach.
3. Yes. Some Muslims are born there, and some become new Muslims.

Building Model Masajid

Using the Muslim World Coloring Book, library books or slides, have the class look at pictures of masajid from many lands. Working in groups, have each make a different masjid and decorate it.

Materials:

> shoe-boxes with lids
> corrugated boxboard for bases (use two-ply or glue two pieces)
> cardboard tubes (mailing, plastic or aluminum wrap, tissue rolls)
> plastic detergent bottle necks and parts
> construction paper or thin cardboard
> tissue paper or acetate (optional)
> fabric scraps
> crayons
> scissors
> white glue
> poster paints
>
> mat knife (for teacher's use only)
> stapler (for teacher's use only)

Using shoe boxes as the basic form for each masjid, have the children add paper cut-outs and cardboard tubes as towers, minarets and columns. Plastic detergent bottle parts serve as domes on the box lid. With the teacher's help, these can be stapled on using tab extensions left on the neck (see illustration). Have each group draw windows and doors on the box sides; the teacher can cut these with a mat knife. Tissue paper may be pasted over the windows if desired. Decorate inside the box with crayons or cover the floor of the masjid with fabric scraps. Paint the outside of the masjid. The group may wish to decorate the cardboard base with pools and gardens.

When complete, place a flashlight or holiday lights inside the box and close the lid. The light will shine through the windows with a dramatic effect.

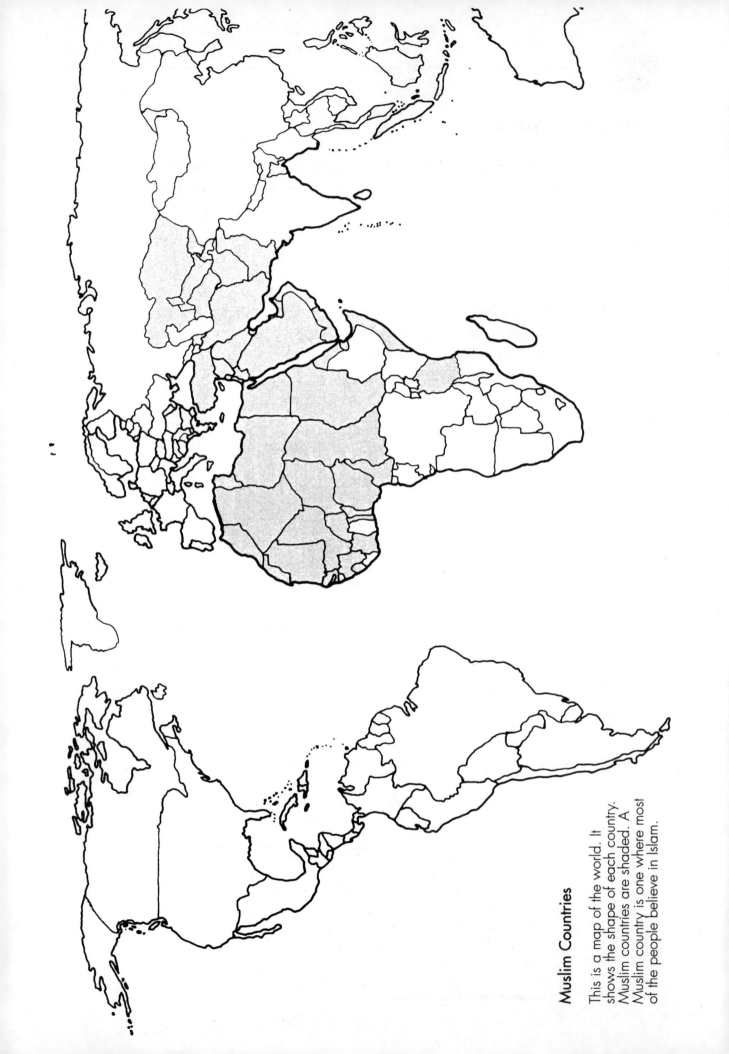

Muslim Countries

This is a map of the world. It shows the shape of each country. Muslim countries are shaded. A Muslim country is one where most of the people believe in Islam.

Review Activity

Arrange these items under the correct heading.

praying each day	helping needy people
eating rice or bread	wearing white clothes
obeying mother and father	going to a picnic

CUSTOM	LAW

Sentence Cut-Ups

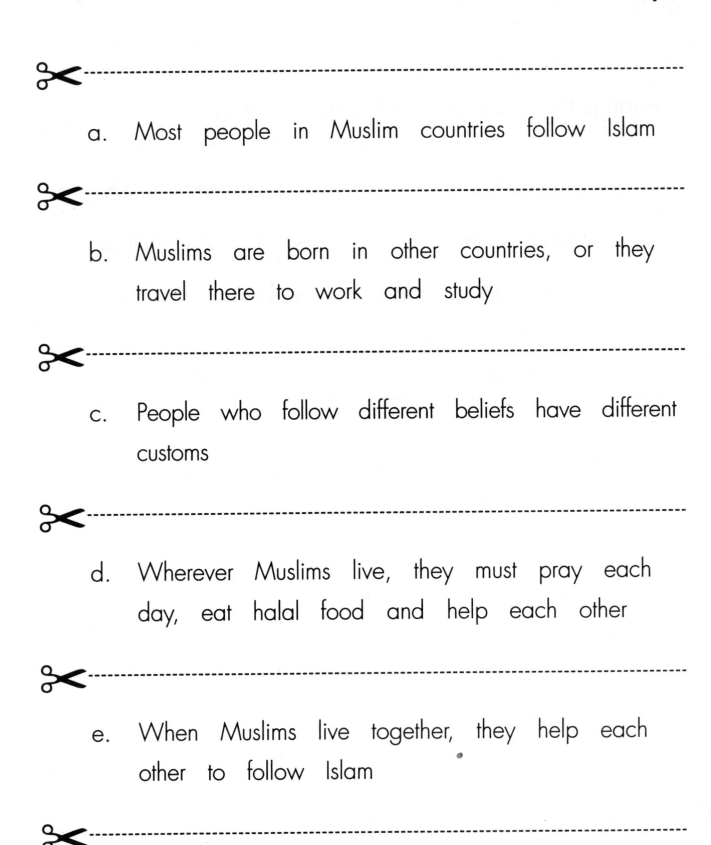

a. Most people in Muslim countries follow Islam

b. Muslims are born in other countries, or they travel there to work and study

c. People who follow different beliefs have different customs

d. Wherever Muslims live, they must pray each day, eat halal food and help each other

e. When Muslims live together, they help each other to follow Islam

Some of My Relatives

Cut out and glue photos of some of your relatives on the circles.
Write what kind of relative is pictured on the line under the photo.

1. Write two sentences about living in a Muslim country.

_____

_____

_____

Write two sentences about Muslims living in the United States.

_____

_____

_____

In each sentence use at least one of the "Words to Know."

2. Find out more:
   a. Which two continents have the most Muslim countries?
   b. Which Muslim country is on a group of islands?

3. A business is a store, office or factory that serves people. Tell what kind of business you might open to serve Muslim families. How would your business help the community? Draw a picture of your business.

4. Answer these riddles! Fill in the blank with one of the "Words To Know" listed below.

masjid   halal   custom   village   pork

a. I am a small community. People here grow crops and raise animals. I am a _____

b. _____ Muslims are not allowed to eat any part of me. I am _____

c. _____I am anything which Allah allowed Muslims to do. I am _____.

d. I am a place where Muslims can pray five times a day. I am a _____ building. I am a _____.

Muslims In Our Community
and Around the World

A. Complete these sentences.
Fill in the ☐ in front of the right word.

1. Which continent has many Muslim countries?

   ☐ Africa   ☐ North America

2. In a Muslim country, most people follow

   ☐ different beliefs and customs   ☐ Islam

3. Which one of these is a custom?

   ☐ wearing a cowboy hat   ☐ helping your parents

4. What are things which Allah (SWT) wants Muslims to do?

   ☐ customs   ☐ Islamic laws

5. Which one of these is a business?

   ☐ a school   ☐ a book store   ☐ a masjid

B. Finish these sentences with the right word.

6. Muslim butchers sell meat and other _____ foods.

7. Muslims use money to help _____ people in the community and in Muslim countries.

C. Name two things that Muslim communities need. Tell how each one helps Muslims to follow Islam.

_____

_____

_____

_____

_____

_____

_____

_____

_____

_____

NOTES